HAL LEONARD KEYBOARD STYLE SERIES

LATIN JAZZ PIANO

THE COMPLETE GUIDE WITH AUDIO!

T0084235

To access audio visit:
www.halleonard.com/mylibrary

1021-9988-0060-7616

BY JOHN VALERIO

ISBN 978-1-4234-1741-5

ABOUT THIS BOOK

All jazz musicians play a number of Latin tunes, but for most cases Latin means a generalized feel and approach, and nothing necessarily specific beyond a straight eighth-note feel. This book offers the jazz pianist a more specific approach to playing Latin jazz piano based on traditional Latin music from Cuba—known as Afro-Cuban—and Brazil. Each differs in its rhythmic approach and feel, and each comes from a different tradition. Whereas the piano is a crucial harmonic and rhythmic instrument in a traditional Afro-Cuban ensemble, the guitar more typically plays that role for a Brazilian ensemble. The jazz pianist, however, often is called on to supply chords and accompaniment rhythms for Brazilian-based jazz when a guitar is not present.

This book does not attempt to instruct the reader in the area of traditional Latin piano playing, but rather in the area of Latin-based jazz piano. The traditions serve as points of departure for a more improvisatory jazz approach. Some of the more popular traditional styles introduced in this book include mambo, cha-cha, bossa nova, and samba. The book addresses the three roles that the jazz pianist typically plays: 1) a member of an accompanying rhythm section, 2) a lead instrument within an ensemble, and 3) a solo instrument. The book is divided into three main sections: Afro-Cuban based jazz piano, Brazilian based jazz piano, and lead sheets for play along.

ABOUT THE AUDIO

The accompanying audio features many of the examples in the book. They are played as solo piano; piano and bass; piano, bass, and lead instrument (vibes); and Latin jazz combo. Lead sheets are provided at the end of the book in order for the reader to play along with the combo tracks. See section 3 for details on the play-along tracks.

ABOUT THE AUTHOR

John Valerio is a pianist, composer, and author from Philadelphia, Pennsylvania. He has performed with several outstanding jazz artists including: Lee Konitz, Jon Faddis, Stanley Clarke, Chris Vadala, John Swana, Gerald Veasley, Winard Harper, Ralph Bowen, Steve Gilmore, and Jan Metzger. He earned a doctorate in Music Composition from Temple University and has written numerous works for a variety of voices, instruments, and ensembles in classical and jazz idioms. *Latin Jazz Piano* is the seventh book he has written for Hal Leonard Corporation. The others are *Stride & Swing Piano*; *Bebop Jazz Piano*; *Post-Bop Jazz Piano*; *Intros, Endings, & Turnaround for Keyboard*; *Jazz Piano: Concepts & Techniques*; and *Playing Keyboard Bass Lines*. His first recording as a leader, *The Altoona Sessions*, was released on ViVadagio Records in 2006, and a new CD featuring all original tunes including several Latin tunes will be released in 2010. Dr. Valerio currently teaches at the University of South Carolina and Newberry College.

INTRODUCTION: WHAT IS LATIN JAZZ?

Latin music has been associated with jazz from the very beginnings of the genre in New Orleans, around 1900. Jelly Roll Morton, the first great jazz pianist and composer/arranger, spoke of the "Spanish tinge" as a crucial element in jazz. He was referring to the habanera rhythm (♩. ♩. ♩). This rhythm was played by Morton and others in the earliest days of jazz and was most famously featured in the middle section of WC Handy's "St. Louis Blues," published in 1914. The habanera rhythm was a key feature of the Cuban *danzón*, which was an important forerunner to more modern Cuban music.

Latin music and jazz share common roots and both are mixtures of African and European musical elements. Form and harmony come from Europe, and rhythmic concepts come from Africa. Latin music also has more direct influence from Spain and Portugal. The proximity of the major ports of New Orleans and Havana led to the exporting and importing of jazz and Latin music, and both influenced each other in the Twentieth Century.

Cuba became a major center for the style known as Afro-Cuban music. Often the term "Afro-Caribbean" is used today to be more inclusive of dominant centers such as Puerto Rico. *Salsa*, the dominant modern style of Afro-Caribbean music, comes largely from Puerto Rico and New York City as well as Cuba. Cuban music, however, played the key role in the first significant merger of jazz and Latin music in the 1930s, and especially in the 1940s. Various big bands of the Swing era incorporated some Cuban influenced dance music in the 1930s, but the real confluence came in the 1940s when Dizzy Gillespie merged Afro-Cuban music with bebop. Dizzy hired Chano Pozo and other Cuban musicians in an effort to merge the two genres. The experiment had some success despite the conflicting rhythmic conceptions. The key difference was the concept of the *clave* in Afro-Cuban music. The *clave* is an underlying rhythm that organizes the surface rhythms of the music. It is often compared to the "swing" feeling associated with much jazz. The concept of the clave is crucial for Afro-Cuban styles, but foreign to most jazz musicians. Latin jazz became more commonplace in the 1950s, and several groups, including those led by George Shearing and Cal Tjader, incorporated the clave concept along with some Cuban musicians. Most jazz musicians, however, played various Latin jazz tunes without regard to the clave.

In regard to Afro-Cuban (Afro-Caribbean) music, the term "Latin jazz" can refer to two different kinds of music: *LATIN Jazz* (based on the clave) and *Latin JAZZ* (not based on the clave). The Afro-Cuban section of this book serves as an introduction to the concept of the clave for jazz musicians who may not be familiar with it. Some of the major LATIN Jazz pianists include Eddie Palmieri, Chucho Valdez, and Michel Camilo. Pianists who play Latin JAZZ include Horace Silver, George Shearing, Claire Fisher, Vince Guaraldi, and Chick Corea. The piano is a crucial member of any Afro-Cuban based music.

The 1960s brought a whole new sound and style to jazz based on a new music from Brazil. It was called "bossa nova" and blended elements of *samba*—a traditional Brazilian music—with jazz. It was sometimes referred to as "jazz samba." Bossa nova took America by storm and entered not only the jazz world but the pop music world as well. Jazz saxophonist, Stan Getz, popularized bossa nova and had several hit records, including "Desafinado" and "The Girl from Ipanema." Both of these songs were written by Antonio Carlos Jobim, who along with Joao Gilberto and others invented the new style in Brazil. Bossa nova's gentle undulating rhythmic underpinnings seemed to appeal to almost everyone and quickly became a standard feature in most jazz and pop musicians' repertoire. Unlike Afro-Cuban music, bossa nova required no extra percussionists and specialized piano parts, and therefore almost anyone and any band could play it. It is safe to say that all jazz musicians play bossa novas, but not all play Afro-Cuban jazz.

Samba-based jazz (from Brazil) became popular in the 1970s through the efforts of Chick Corea and others, and is also a mainstay of most jazz musicians. Samba jazz offered a viable alternative to rock-based fusion jazz, and in some ways its popularity led to an interest in the newer Afro-Cuban styles collectively known as "salsa." Salsa became popular in the late 1970s as a dance music that rivaled disco among many young dancers. Most Afro-Cuban music has usually been called "salsa" ever since.

This book is divided into three sections. The first covers Afro-Cuban (Afro-Caribbean) jazz, the second section deals with Brazilian influenced jazz-bossa nova and samba, and the third contains lead sheets of the tunes and instructions for the play-along tracks.

The Afro-Cuban section contains a chapter on some basic concepts of traditional Afro-Cuban music, including the *clave*, *tumbao*, and *montuno*. Also, there is a chapter on typical piano voicing used in Afro-Cuban music Latin jazz in general. Next is a chapter on typical comping patterns used in various Afro-Cuban styles such as mambo, cha-cha, etc. The last chapter in this section features tunes written in these various styles and arranged for lead instrument, piano and bass, piano lead, and piano solo.

The next section on Brazilian-related jazz begins with a chapter on the many varied rhythms typically used in comping for bossa novas and sambas, and concludes with a chapter featuring tunes arranged in the same ways as the first section.

The third section contains lead sheets of all the tunes so the reader can play and improvise on them along with the accompanying audio. The reader is encouraged to continually change the way he or she plays these tunes and apply the principles found in this book to other tunes in the Latin jazz repertoire.

CONTENTS

Section 1

AFRO-CUBAN BASED JAZZ PIANO

Chapter 1
AFRO-CUBAN BASICS

The Clave

Most Afro-Cuban/salsa music is built upon the clave. The *clave* is a rhythmic feel superimposed on the pulse. It organizes the rhythmic flow of the music and all rhythmic elements, including melody and harmony, and how they relate to the pulse. It received its name from the "claves," a traditional Latin instrument composed of two wooden cylindrical sticks. It is the claves player that most typically states the clave rhythm when it is played by striking the two sticks together. Technically, the clave is a two-measure pattern that consists of five strikes: two strikes occur in one measure and three in the other. Thus the clave pattern contains a "2-side" and a "3-side." The clave pattern can begin with either the 2-side or the 3-side. Latin musicians refer to it as a "2:3 clave" or a "3:2 clave." Sometimes these are written also as "2/3" and "3/2," or as "2-3" and "3-2." The terms "forward clave" and "reverse clave" are also used ("3:2" = forward, and "2:3" = reverse clave). Once the clave is established, it repeats throughout a performance, however the clave may or may not be directly played or heard. The important aspect of the clave is that all rhythmic events are based upon it. It is always felt but not necessarily heard.

Most non-Latin jazz musicians are unfamiliar with the concept of the clave, but it is as important to the rhythmic feeling of Afro-Cuban based music as the concept of swing feel is to traditional jazz musicians.

There are two clave patterns used in Afro-Cuban music and salsa: the *son clave* and the *rumba clave*. They both can occur in a 2:3 or 3:2 direction. The 2:3 direction is often referred to as the *reverse clave*, but is shown first here because it is more common.

Son Clave

2:3 Son Clave

3:2 Son Clave

Rumba Clave

2:3 Rumba Clave

3:2 Rumba Clave

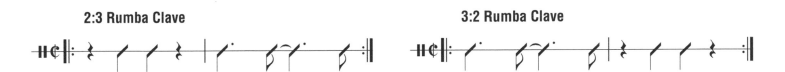

The clave may or may not be played during a performance. Even when it is not, it is still felt, and all other rhythms relate to it. Sometimes the pulse is felt in "four" and sometimes in "two." The clave should be felt in relation to both the quarter note and the half note. The son clave is more common and is shown on the following page.

Son Clave

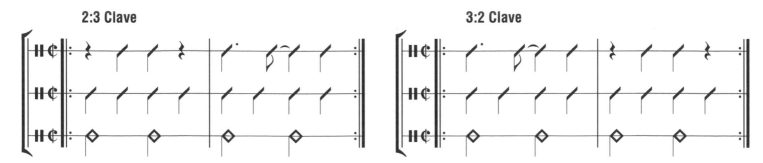

One should practice feeling the clave by tapping it with one hand while tapping quarter notes with the other hand (see example A, below), and then by tapping the clave with the half-note pulse with the other hand (see example B).

A.

B.

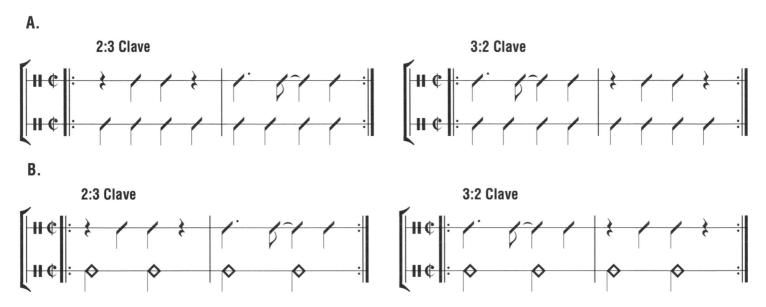

Afro-Cuban and all Latin genres are based on a *layered rhythmic concept*: complex rhythms are created through the simultaneous playing of several different repetitive rhythmic patterns. At the most basic layer is the half-note pulse, then the quarter-note subdivision of the pulse, then the eighth-note subdivision, and then the clave itself. In most situations, every eighth note is played by one or more instruments. This makes for a composite rhythm of steady eighth notes. Interest and variety are created by the separate rhythms, accents, and sounds of each individual instrument.

A typical Cuban percussion section part for a mambo might look like this:

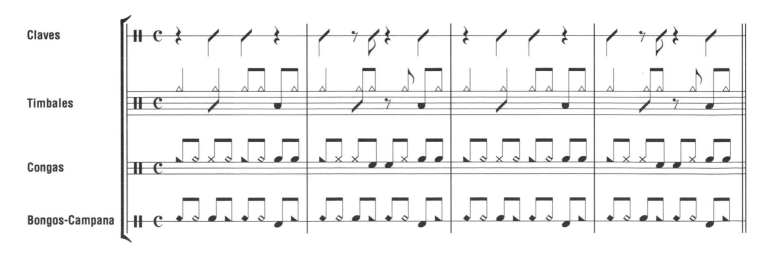

The rumba clave should be practiced in relation to the half-note and quarter-note pulse in the same way as the son clave from the previous example.

Rumba Clave

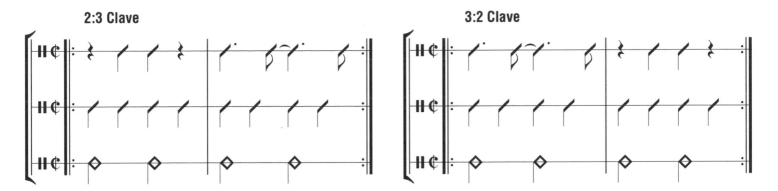

Some Afro-Cuban music is played in 6/8 meter. The 6/8 clave is usually played in the forward direction, but could be played in the reverse direction as well. It features one measure of four strikes and one measure of three strikes. The forward direction (4:3) is shown first. The 6/8 clave should be practiced against the eighth note and dotted quarter-note pulse.

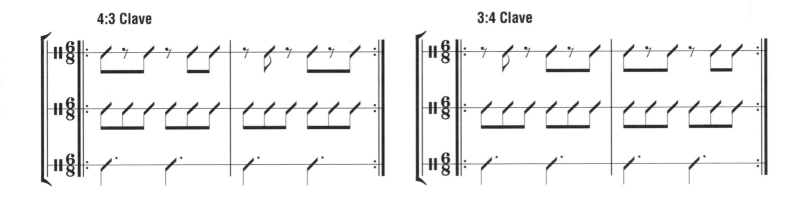

The Tumbao

The typical bass part in Cuban music is usually called the *tumbao*. The word "tumbao" is sometimes used to describe any accompaniment pattern, but is used here to refer to a bass part. In traditional Afro-Cuban music, the bass usually plays the root and fifth of each chord and plays them mostly on the "and" of beat two and on beat four. The note played on beat four anticipates the harmony of the following measure. A typical tumbao part will start on beat one but then mostly will tie over the note from beat four onto each succeeding downbeat. The next example is how a typical tumbao may be played.

TRACK 1

The following is a typical tumbao part when the chords change every two beats.

Countless variations can be applied to the basic tumbao pattern. Below is an example of variations on the basic pattern with two chords lasting four measures each.

The tumbao most often works independently from the clave, thus bass parts tend to be similar regardless of the direction of the clave.

Montuno

In traditional Cuban music the piano typically plays a two-measure repetitive pattern called a *montuno*. Like the word "tumbao," the word "montuno" can be confusing. It may refer to an open vamp-like solo section of a tune, any piano accompaniment part, or the syncopated arpeggio-like piano accompaniment typically played in much Afro-Cuban music. The term "montuno" will be used in this book in reference to the latter usage shown in the following example.

The most commonly used rhythm for a 2:3 clave is shown below.

2:3 Clave

The rhythm of each measure will switch for a 3:2 clave.

3:2 Clave

Montunos are usually played legato and the rhythms shown above should more properly be written without rests. The montuno rhythms should be interpreted the same way, with or without rests. Notice the 3:2 clave pattern in the second example starts with a hit on the first beat. The montuno is often started this way, but from then on, this note is tied over from the last note of the pattern.

2:3 Clave

3:2 Clave

These exact same rhythms also may be rewritten as follows:

2:3 Clave

3:2 Clave

Even though they are not always adhered to, montuno parts are often easier to read with rests.

The following shows the relationship among the montuno rhythms, and the quarter-note and the half-note pulse.

2:3 Clave　　　　　　　　　　　　　　**3:2 Clave**

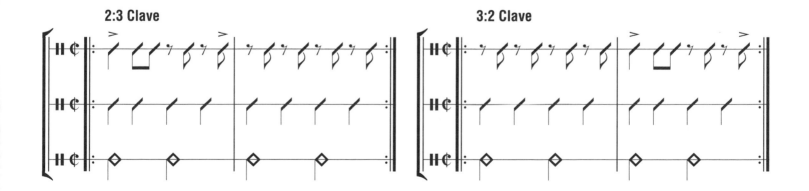

The following shows the relationship among the montuno rhythms, the clave, and the half-note pulse.

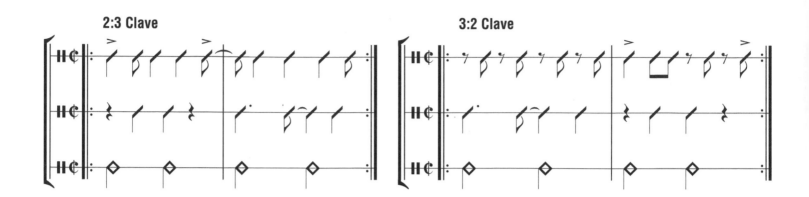

The following is the basis for a typical montuno pattern on a G7 chord.

TRACK 4

This pattern can be played in octaves, with both hands.

TRACK 5

Thirds are often added to enrich the sound.

TRACK 6

Octaves are often added to the right-hand part as well.

TRACK 7

The basic montuno pattern can be applied to a variety of chord progressions. A simple I-IV-V-IV montuno (in C major) follows.

TRACK 8

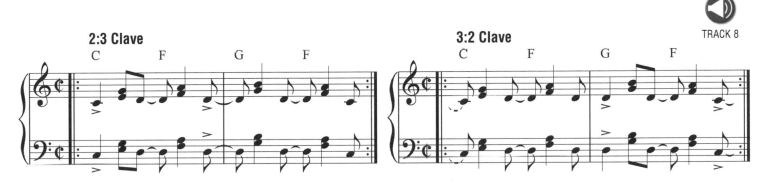

Montunos often use octaves in place of single notes.

TRACK 9

The following shows two different montunos for the same I-IV-V-IV chord progression.

TRACK 10

A.

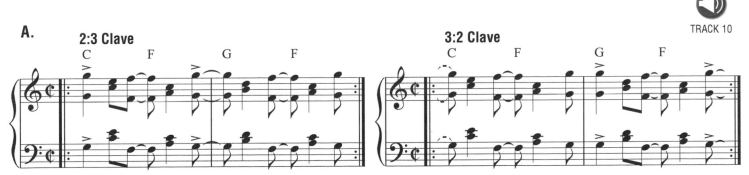

B.

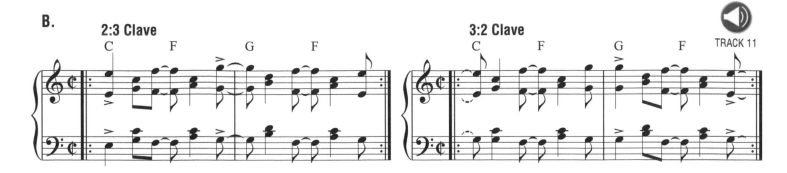

Notes for montunos can easily be chosen from standard voicing formulas. Typical voicing formulas for ii–V progressions in C major can be turned into the following montunos.

Montuno

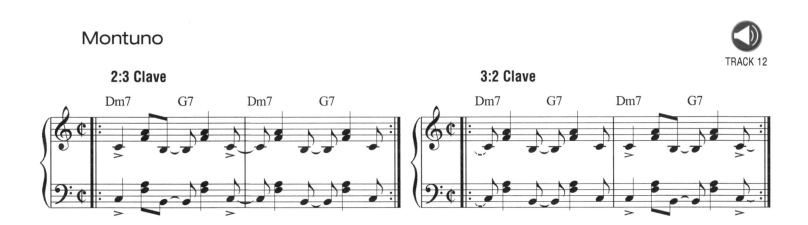

Octaves can be added above the lowest note of each voicing and applied to the montuno.

Montuno

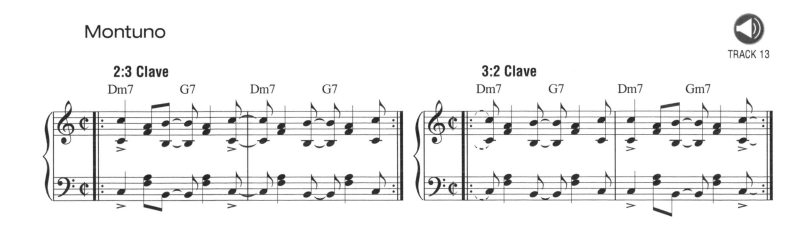

Montunos are typically played on repeating ii–V progressions for solo sections of Afro-Cuban tunes. The next two examples are in F major.

Montuno

TRACK 14

Montuno

TRACK 15

Montunos are also common in minor keys. Here is an example in G minor.

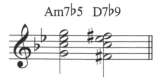

Montuno

TRACK 16

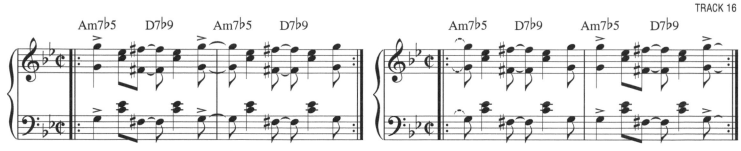

Harmony is sometimes used for variety's sake in playing montunos. Thirds are often employed in place of octaves.

TRACK 17

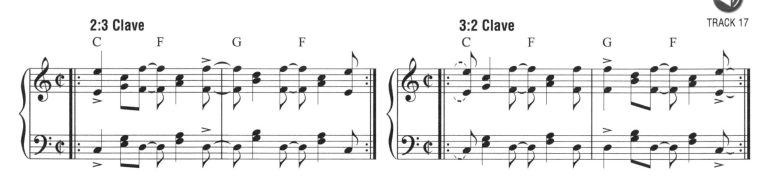

Combined Montuno And Tumbao

Sometimes the pianist may be required to play both montuno and tumbao parts at the same time. This may happen in the absence of a bass player or in solo piano playing. Although this does not happen often, it is a very useful exercise to practice both at the same time. Playing both can be difficult, but by doing it, the pianist may gain a real sense of the rhythmic layers of Afro-Cuban music. It also serves as a great exercise in coordination between the hands, and prepares the pianist for solo playing.

TRACK 18

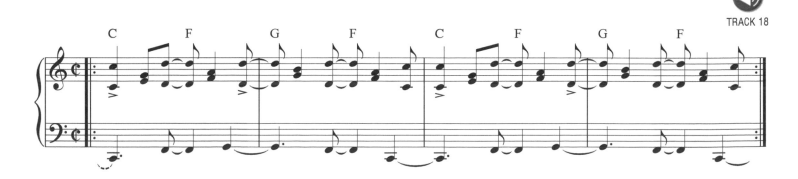

Chapter 2

CHORD VOICINGS

Left-Hand Voicings

Afro-Cuban music tends to favor voicings that produce the most movement in the lowest voice. The left hand usually plays an open three-note rootless voicing around the "middle C" area, and the right hand usually plays bright sounding voicings that often contain triads with octaves and/or fourths, an octave or so higher.

Standard rootless voicings are usually played with three or four notes. The two most common four-note rootless voicing formulas for ii–V–I progressions are shown in the next example for the key C major.

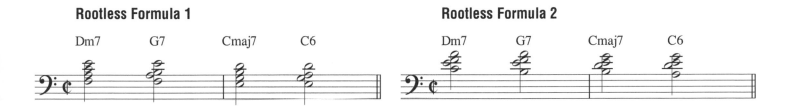

Three-note rootless voicings are derived by dropping one note.

Three-note rootless voicings are more common than four-note voicings, and formula 2 is more common than formula 1. Latin pianists tend to favor the open sounds that the three-note voicings produce, and formula 2, by exposing the "7th–3rd" and "3rd–7th" voice-leading in the lowest notes, emphasizes this important harmonic motion.

Voicings for Two Hands

Triadic upper structures with octaves are very common voicings used in the right hand. Several common procedures for II–V progressions are shown in the next example. All are in the key of G major.

A common II–V voicing formula for two hands is derived by playing three-note rootless formula 2 voicings in the left hand, and a II chord triad with octaves in the right hand. In the following examples in G major, the right hand plays an A minor triad with octaves in three positions.

In the next example, the A minor triad changes to a D major triad for the V chord (D7).

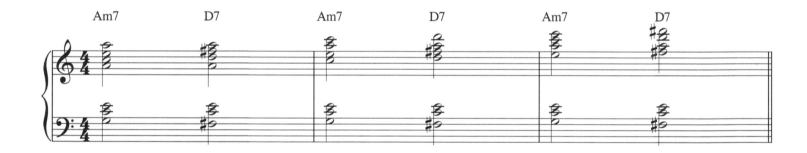

In the following example, a C major triad is played for the ii chord (Am7), and moves to a D major triad for the V chord (D7).

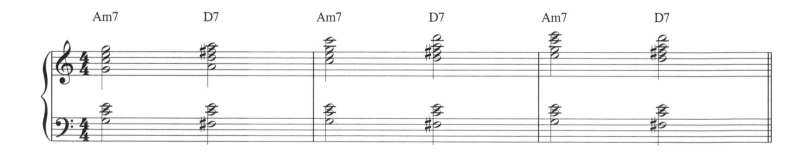

Examples of both types of voicing are shown below as played in a typical *cha-cha*.

The concepts used above can also be applied to ii–V–I progressions.

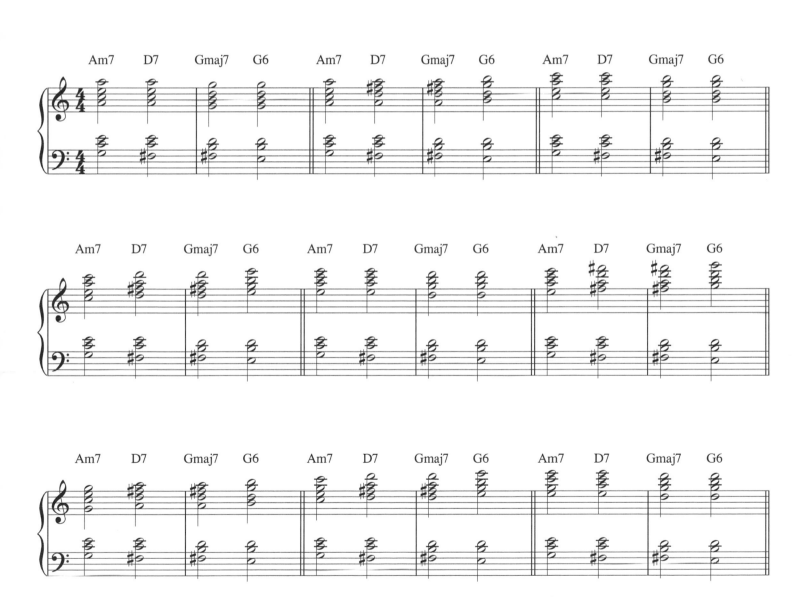

Three-note voicings featuring fourths and fifths are often used in right-hand voicings. Examples for ii–V progressions follow.

These ideas can be applied also to ii–V–I progressions.

Although not as common, Rootless Voicing Formula 1 three-note voicings can be used in the left hand along with the same right-hand upper structures as shown in the following examples.

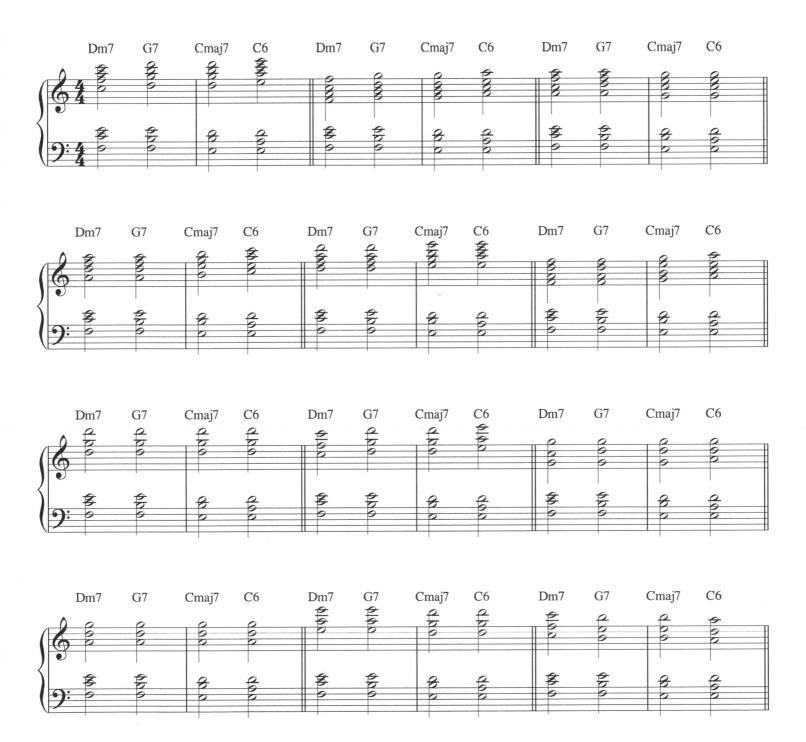

Minor ii-V-i Voicings

The voicing principles used for major ii–V–I progressions can be applied to minor keys in a similar way. Several examples follow.

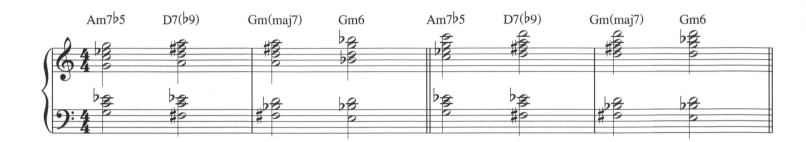

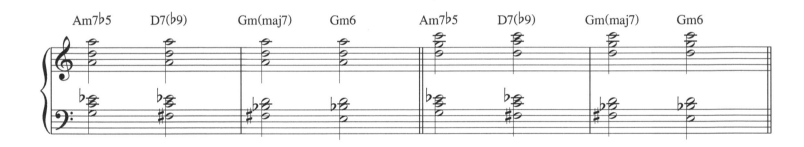

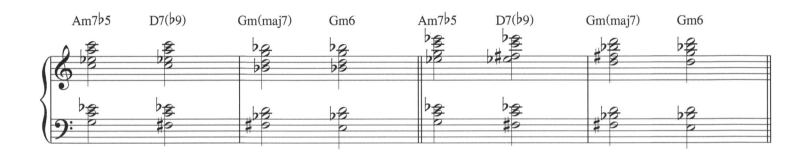

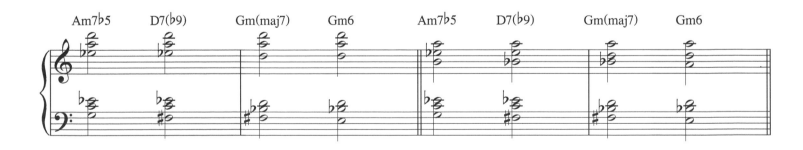

The examples that follow use a Gm7 chord instead of a Gm(maj7) as a i chord in minor. These chords can be used interchangeably in all of the examples.

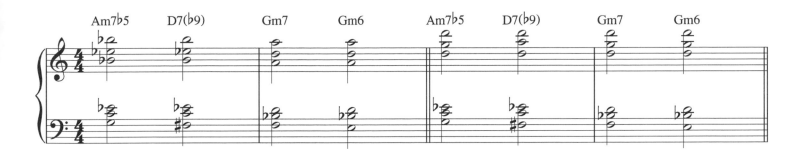

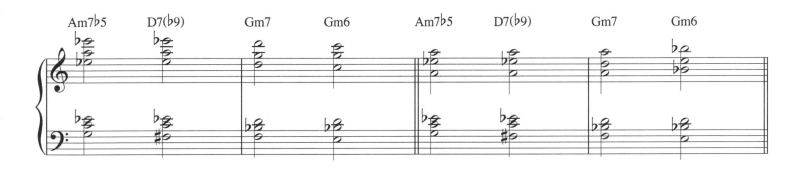

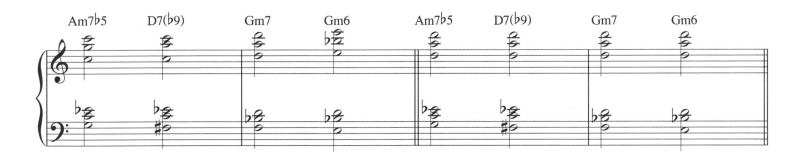

Although three-note left-hand voicings are more common in Afro-Cuban music, four-note voicings are used and can be used with all of the right-hand voicings shown previously. A few examples follow.

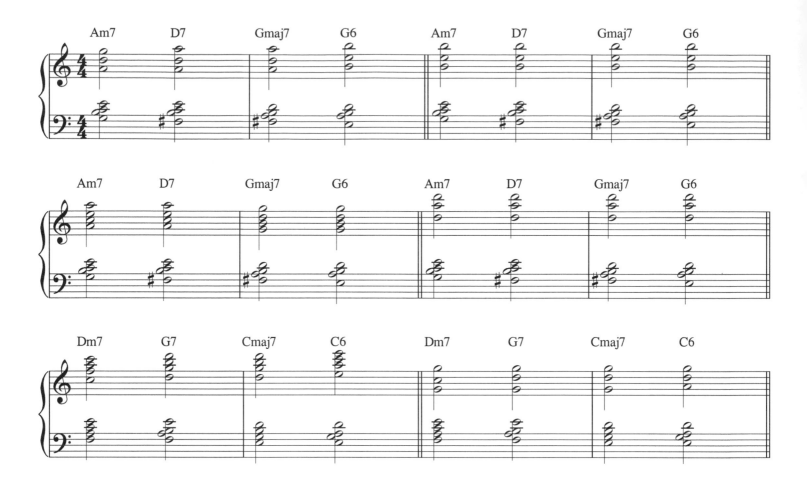

Latin jazz pianists generally use three- or four-note voicings in the left hand when playing melodies with the right hand. There are numerous examples of this in the chapters that follow.

Chapter 3
AFRO-CUBAN COMPING

The pianist plays a key role in the Afro-Cuban and Latin jazz rhythm section. The pianist's main functions are both rhythmic and harmonic. This chapter will present some of the ways that the piano is used in various types and styles of Afro-Cuban music, including salsa and Latin jazz. The pianist's comping usually consists of bright chords in well-defined rhythmic patterns or montuno-like patterns.

Mambo

The mambo evolved from the Cuban *danzón*, which is a traditional style of Cuban music and dance. The mambo began in the 1930s as an added section to the *danzón* featuring montuno-like vamps. The mambo soon became its own style and continues to be a popular music and dance style. Mambos are characterized by fast tempos and strong rhythmic accents.

Montuno Comping

Various montuno-like accompaniments can be played for a mambo. A few variations on the standard montuno pattern follow. All are in the 2:3 clave.

TRACK 19

The next one has more continuous motion.

TRACK 20

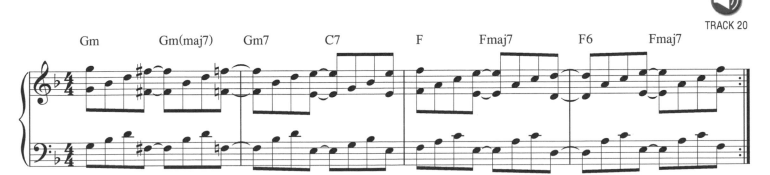

This pattern combines elements of the previous two examples.

TRACK 21

Here is another rhythmic variation.

TRACK 22

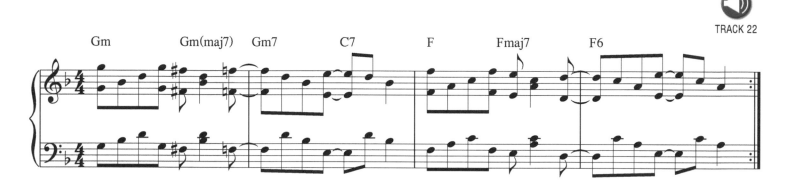

More on-the-beat rhythms are displayed in the following example.

TRACK 23

The next pattern features a dotted quarter-note rhythm on the first beat.

TRACK 24

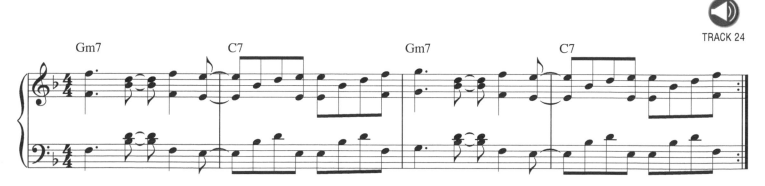

Chordal Comping

The pianist may also comp chords for mambos. Two examples follow.

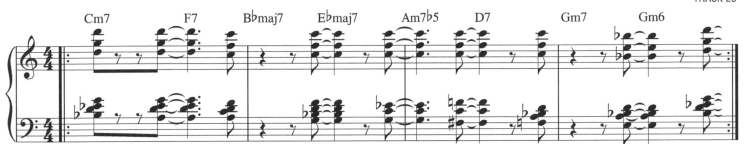

Cha-Cha-Cha

The cha-cha-cha is also known as the cha-cha. It evolved as a kind of slowed down *danzón*/mambo and became an international craze in the 1950s. The tempos are usually moderate, and the pianist generally plays one of several well-defined rhythmic patterns.

Chordal Comping

There are several approaches that one can apply to comping for a cha-cha. The first is to comp full chords with both hands in a well-defined rhythm that complements the dance that goes with the music. Two common approaches follow.

The next three patterns feature constant off-beat chords in the left hand and on-the-beat chords or mostly on-the-beat chords in the right hand.

Montuno Comping

Another common way to accompany a cha-cha is to play montuno-like patterns as in the following three examples.

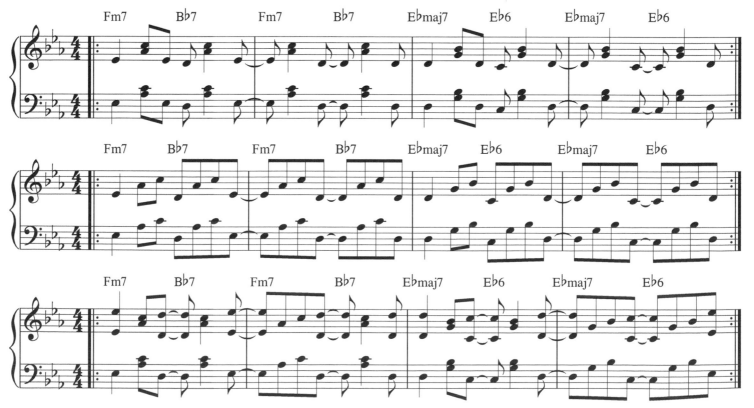

A more random-like approach is also possible.

Guaracha

The *guaracha* evolved from songs performed in Cuban comic operas in the 19th century. Today the term "guaracha" usually refers to a medium-tempo Afro-Cuban groove. The piano parts are similar to other Afro-Cuban styles.

The following pattern works well with a medium-tempo guaracha.

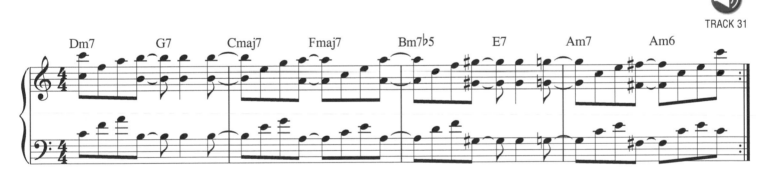

Salsa

The term "salsa" can be confusing. The word was first used in the 1970s to describe what was essentially the Cuban son. The son was a popular peasant music from the 1800s in Cuba. The concept of the montuno comes from the son and much of modern salsa and Afro-Cuban music is based on it. On the other hand, salsa can refer to Afro-Cuban based music that evolved on the East Coast of the U.S. and Puerto Rico from the 1970s. Any changes in modern salsa do not really affect the pianist's playing, and the pianist basically plays in one of the styles demonstrated previously in this chapter.

The following five examples (A–E) show some typical comping patterns and styles for contemporary salsa playing. These can be used in a variety of styles and tempos.

TRACK 32

TRACK 33

TRACK 34

TRACK 35

E.   3:2

Latin Jazz

Although all of the examples in this chapter apply to Latin jazz in general, there are some comping patterns that relate more specifically to a style labeled as "Latin jazz" as opposed to salsa, etc.

Montuno Comping

The following two examples feature a montuno-like right hand with a chordal left hand.

A.   2:3

Chordal Comping

The next example features chordal comping in both hands.

The next chapter shows many examples of comping in the context of Afro-Cuban based tunes.

Chapter 4
CHARACTERISTIC AFRO-CUBAN TUNES

There are many diverse genres within the Afro-Cuban idiom. This chapter will offer examples from the ones that jazz musicians use the most. Each tune is written in two different ways: 1) as a score for lead instrument, piano accompaniment, and bass, and 2) as a piano lead version as would be played with a rhythm section.

Mambo

"Mambo Mia" is a bright mambo that features montuno-like comping as well as chordal comping. There is also a montuno solo section, which is common in mambos.

Mambo Mia

TRACK 40

Lead Instrument, Piano, and Bass

Montuno Solo Section
Play 8 times

D.C. al Fine

Mambo Mia

TRACK 41

Piano Lead

2:3 Clave
Fast Mambo ♩ = 200

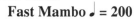

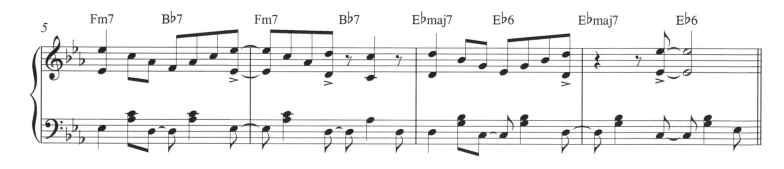

Cha-Cha-Chá

"Alacha" is a medium tempo cha-cha that features a typical chordal cha-cha piano accompaniment as well as a montuno-like comping section. Notice the opening vamp that serves to set up the feel and groove of the cha-cha.

Alacha

TRACK 42

Lead Instrument, Piano, and Bass

2:3 Clave
Cha-Cha ♩ = 154

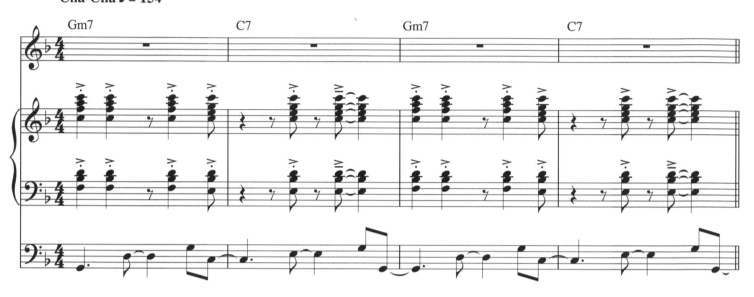

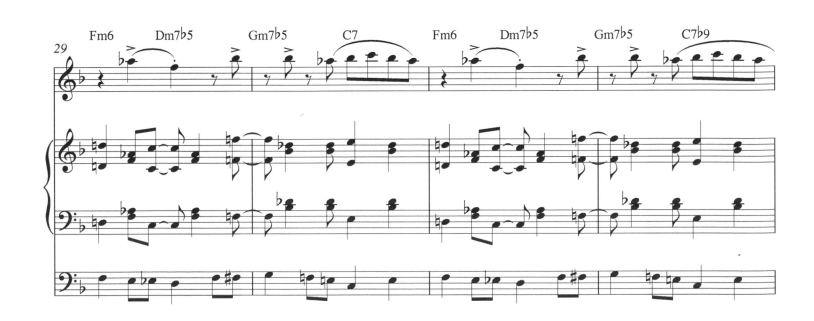

This next version of "Alacha" is written for piano to be played with a rhythm section. The left-hand comping is similar to the two-hand comping used before.

Alacha

TRACK 43

Piano Lead

2:3 Clave
Cha-Cha ♩ = 154

Guaracha

"Speranza" is a medium tempo guaracha in a 3:2 clave. The piano comping is chordal and based largely on the clave rhythm itself. Notice how the opening bass vamp sets up the mood and feel of the tune.

Speranza

TRACK 44

Lead Instrument, Piano, and Bass

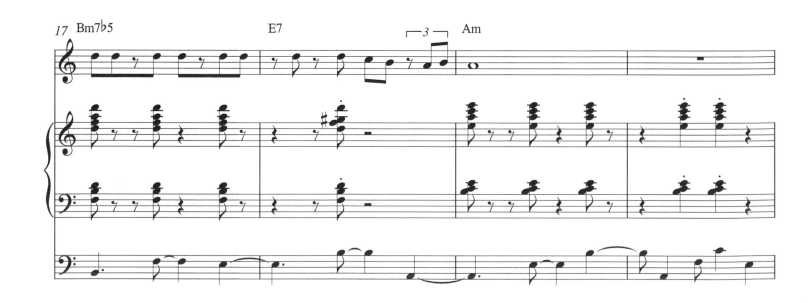

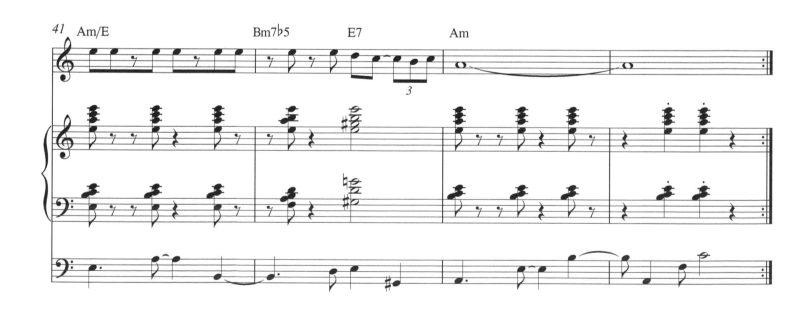

This next version of "Speranza" is for piano lead as it would be played with a rhythm section. The left-hand comping is derived rhythmically from the two-hand comping used in the previous example.

Speranza

Piano Lead

3:2 Clave
Guaracha ♩ = 172

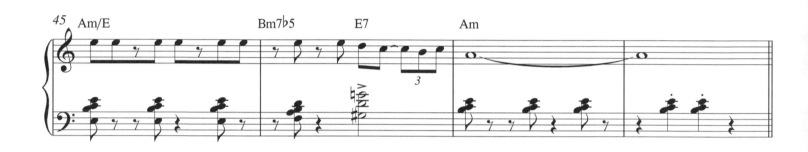

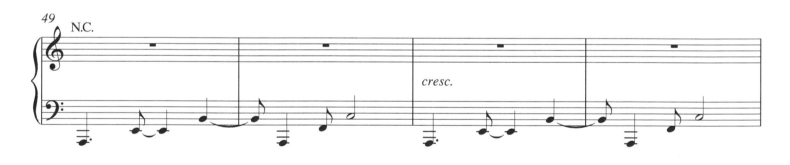

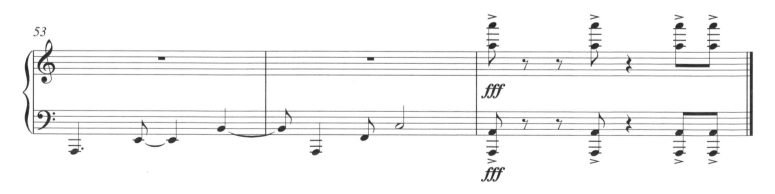

Afro-Jazz Waltz

"Felice Triplice" is an Afro-jazz waltz in triple meter. It is inspired by Mongo Santamaria's "Afro Blue," also made famous by John Coltrane. The tune is based on the reverse 6/8 clave, but written in 3/4. The eighth note has now become a quarter note and the clave is spread out over four measures rather than two measures (see p. 9). The first part of the tune features chordal comping, and the second part features montuno-like comping based on the same chord changes. In this book, "Felice Triplice" is written only in the full score form. The reader should also derive and play a piano lead version based on what was learned and observed in the previous examples in this chapter.

(see p. 9)

Felice Triplice

TRACK 46

Lead Instrument, Piano, and Bass

Solo Piano

Playing solo Afro-Cuban based Latin jazz piano requires a good sense of independence. The pianist must play melody, comp, and play bass, all at the same time. In order to accomplish this, a compromise must be made between the comping and bass parts. Various notes and rhythms have to be left out in order to accommodate each part. Decisions in this regard are often determined by the melody being played at any particular moment.

In the following version of "Alacha," the left hand plays a minimal bass part for the first section of the tune, while maintaining most of the cha-cha comp rhythm used in the previous versions. Notice also the added chords with some melody notes in the right-hand part. For the second part of the tune, the left hand plays the montuno part and then the bass part from the other versions.

Alacha

TRACK 47

Solo Piano

Section 2

BRAZILIAN BASED JAZZ PIANO

Chapter 5
BRAZILIAN COMPING

The pianist usually has a different role in a Brazilian rhythm section from that in an Afro-Cuban one. The piano is a crucial instrument defining the rhythm, harmony, and sound of an Afro-Cuban rhythm section. In a Brazilian jazz rhythm section, however, the guitar plays this role. The piano in a Brazilian jazz rhythm section usually will play sparsely and decoratively when a guitar is present, but will assume the guitar's role when a guitar is absent. The examples in this chapter are based on playing without a guitar.

Voicings

Voicings used for Brazilian jazz are virtually the same as used for all modern jazz—primarily rootless voicings. The voicings shown for Afro-Cuban music in chapter 2 can be used for Brazilian jazz as well, but the Brazilian sound is more subdued and more harmonically colorful than the typical Afro-Cuban sound, and richer, fuller chords are used more often. This results in more use of four-note rootless voicings rather than the three-note voicings. (See this author's book *Post-Bop Jazz Piano*, published by Hal Leonard Corporation, for more on modern voicings.)

Brazilian Clave

Although not as crucial, pervasive, and determining as the Afro-Cuban clave, a Brazilian clave does exist. Some debate its significance, but it does seem to organize some Brazilian rhythms.

3:2 Brazilian Clave   **2:3 Brazilian Clave**

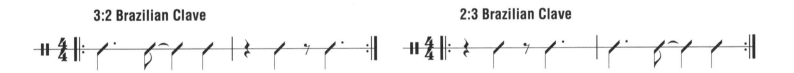

Most Brazilian jazz is very flexible in its rhythmic backgrounds, and most jazz musicians are unaware of any clave at all, but it can be useful in organizing background rhythms and distinguishing Brazilian from Afro-Cuban jazz.

Bossa Nova

Bossa nova was invented in the 1950s and spread to America in the early 1960s. It basically combines elements of the traditional Brazilian music called samba with cool jazz. The lush harmonies of '50s and '60s jazz combine well with the underlying, undulating rhythms of bossa nova. These rhythms are freer, and less structured and repetitive than those of the traditional samba. Comping for bossa novas is usually more flexible and fluid than Afro-Cuban comping. In this regard, it is more similar to jazz comping.

Bossa nova rhythms tend to be based on two models. The first model is based on the so-called "3:2 Brazilian clave." This is a standard two-measure pattern that is typically played by a drummer. It features an accent on the "and" of two in the first measure.

Bossa Nova Comping Model #1

TRACK 48

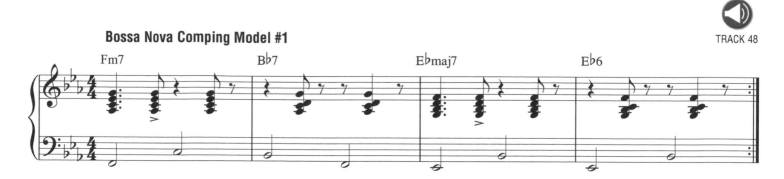

The second comping model features an accent on the second beat of the first measure. This is more in line with the "reverse 2:3 Brazilian clave." Notice that the chord played on the "and" of four anticipates the new chord if the chord changes.

Bossa Nova Comping Model #2

TRACK 49

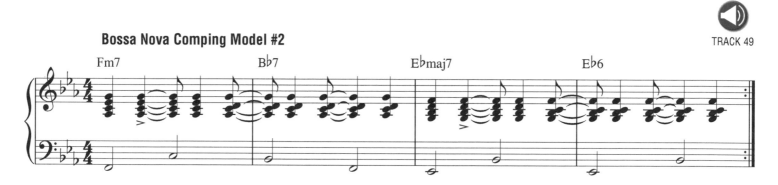

Practice Comping

All of the patterns in this section will be written for the right hand and a simple half-note bass line. (However, these right-hand rhythms can and should also be played with the left hand alone.) Playing the bass part in the left hand will help solidify the pulse along with the syncopated right-hand patterns.

The right-hand part then should be played in the left hand.

The reader may then apply the pattern to other chord progressions and tunes. An example follows.

Bossa Comping with One Hand

There are a seemingly endless number of bossa nova patterns. Several possibilities based on typical bossa chord progressions follow. All should be practiced, as demonstrated in the previous examples, with the right-hand comp rhythms along with the bass and with the same comp rhythms in the left hand alone.

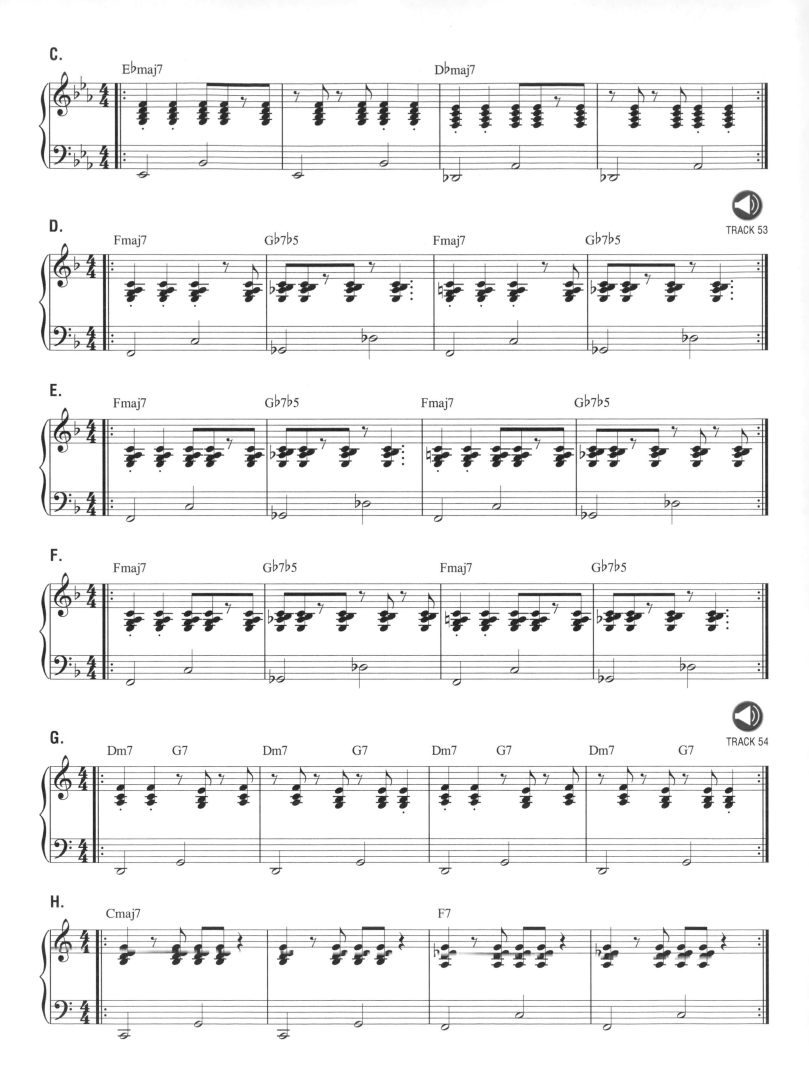

O.

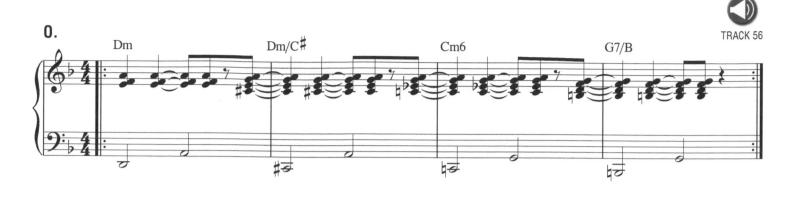

P.

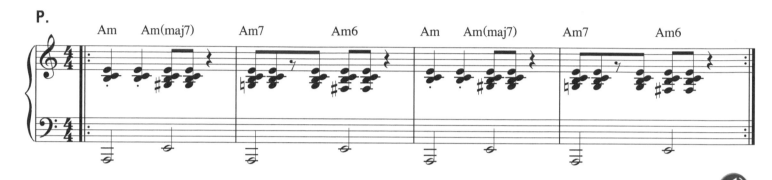

Q.

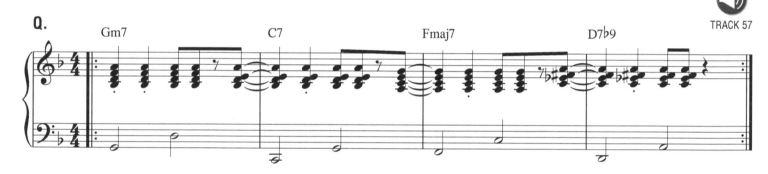

R.

S.

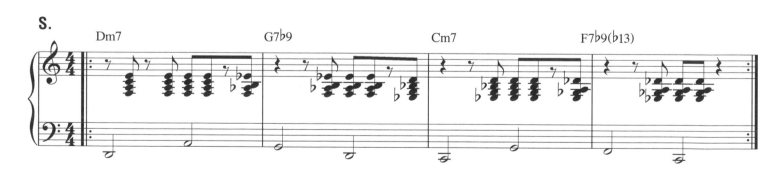

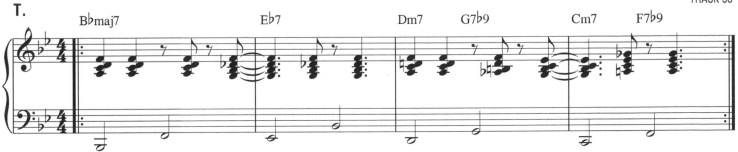

Bossa Comping with Two Hands

The pianist has several options when accompanying other instruments.

Comping patterns are rarely played strictly and repetitively; rather, the rhythms played are usually flexible and flowing, and are placed to fit within the overall rhythmic groove. Like other styles of jazz comping, rhythms and voicing are usually decided in the moment.

Two-Handed Synchronized Comping

One way to comp is to play identical rhythms with both hands.

TRACK 59

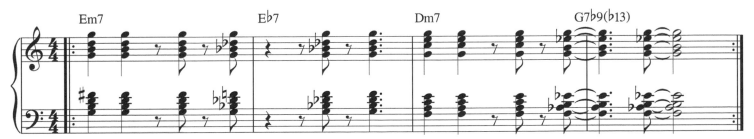

Two-Handed Non-Synchronized Comping

Often the right hand can play sustained chords while the left hand comps in a more rhythmic style. Two examples follow.

TRACK 60

A.

B.

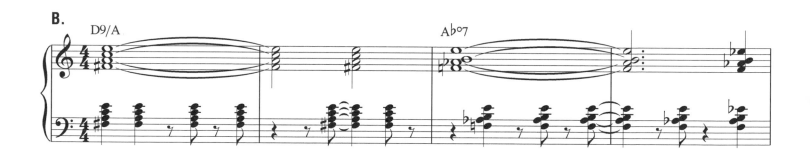

In the next example, the right hand plays more of a linear melodic line against the left-hand rhythm.

TRACK 61

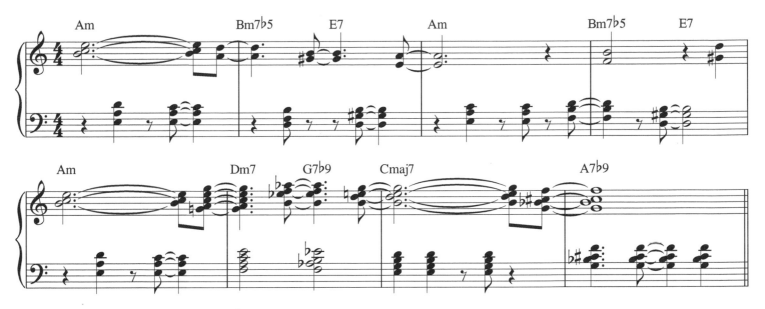

Samba

As far as the jazz pianist is concerned, the main differences between a samba and bossa nova are tempo and meter. Sambas are generally faster and felt in "two" rather than "four." Practically all of the bossa comping patterns described previously can be used for sambas if they are felt in cut time and played at faster tempos. Samba patterns, like the bossa nova patterns, can be thought of as fitting into the Brazilian clave in either direction. (See the beginning of this chapter.) The following are some patterns associated more specifically with the samba.

One-Measure Comping Patterns

Sambas often feature one-measure repeating rhythmic patterns.

TRACK 62

A.

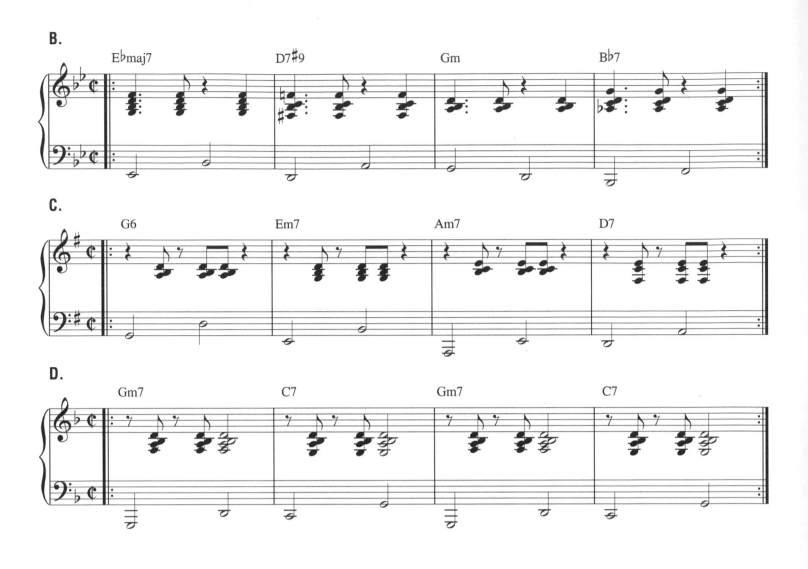

Two- and Four-Measure Patterns

Two- and four-measure repeating patterns are also common.

TRACK 63

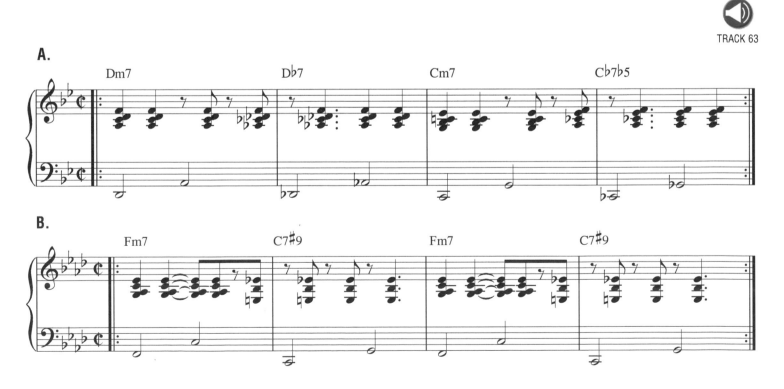

TRACK 64

TRACK 65

H.

Combined Comping Patterns

After practicing the previous bossa nova and samba patterns the reader should play through these examples or various tunes by improvising and mixing up comping voicings and rhythms.

Chapter 6

CHARACTERISTIC BRAZILIAN TUNES

Bossa Nova

Generally there are two types of bossa nova tunes. Some are characterized by flowing melodic lines featuring many long-held notes. Other tunes are characterized by more rhythmic melodies, with faster note values. Both types are played at all tempos.

Medium Bossa

"Bozza Nozza" is a bossa of the first type. It has many long-held notes, rich harmonies, and unexpected harmonic turns. These characteristics are typical of bossa tunes. The first version, shown in the next example, is for a lead instrument with piano and bass accompaniment. Notice how the comping rhythms complement the melody and lock into a bossa rhythmic feel without constant repetition. The bass part is given to show how the overall composite rhythm of all the parts works.

Bozza Nozza

TRACK 87

One can play a solo piano accompaniment to this tune by playing the bass part in the left hand and the left-hand chords in the right hand.

This next version of "Bozza Nozza" is for piano playing the lead with left-hand comping as one might with a rhythm section.

Bozza Nozza

TRACK 67

Piano Lead

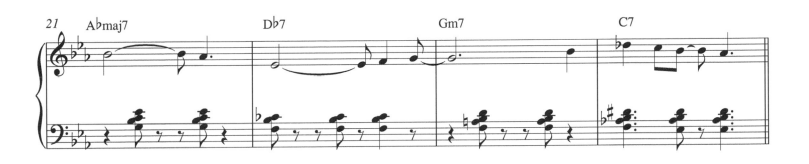

Up-Tempo Bossa

"Cosa Nuova" is a bossa of the second type—one with a more active, rhythmic melody. The following is a version for lead instrument, piano accompaniment, and bass.

Cosa Nuova

TRACK 68

Lead Instrument, Piano, and Bass

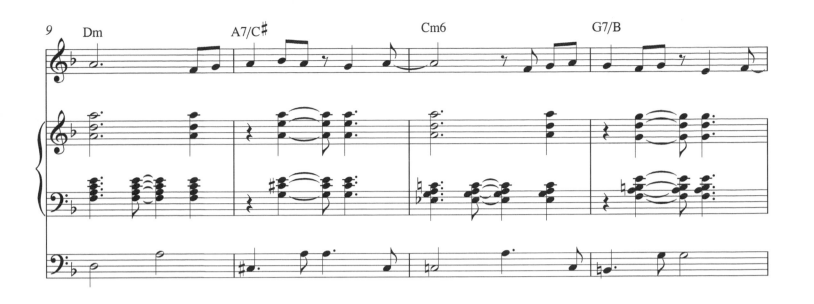

This next version of "Cosa Nuova" is for piano playing the lead, with left-hand comping as one might engage in when playing with a rhythm section.

Cosa Nuova

TRACK 69

Piano Lead

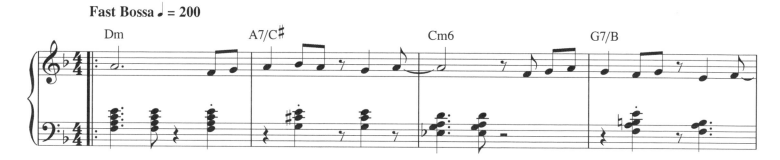

Samba

The *samba* is the most important and characteristic of all traditional Brazilian styles. Although bossa nova is derived from samba, they differ mainly with regard to meter. Sambas are generally played in cut time (2/2) and bossas are generally played in common time (4/4). Sambas are generally faster than bossas, but in some jazz situations, there is little to no distinction between the two, and they are treated and interpreted similarly.

"Samba Maria" is an up-tempo samba that features an active rhythmic melody. This version is for lead instrument, piano, and bass. Notice the way the repetitive one-measure comping pattern is used along with other rhythmic patterns.

Samba Maria

TRACK 70

Lead Instrument, Piano, and Bass

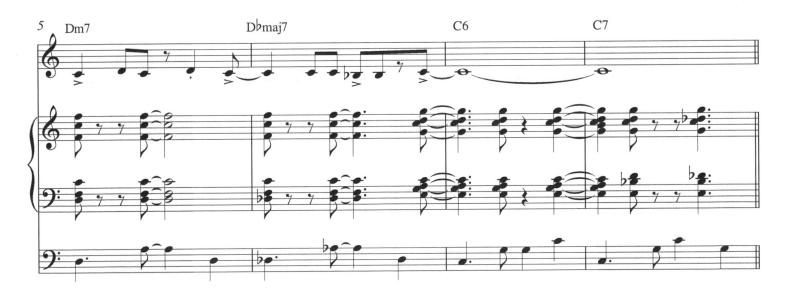

This next version of "Samba Maria" is for piano as it would be played with a rhythm section. Notice the root voicings in the left hand. They are used to reinforce the descending chromatic bass line and work well with the low melody in the right hand.

Samba Maria

TRACK 71

Piano Lead

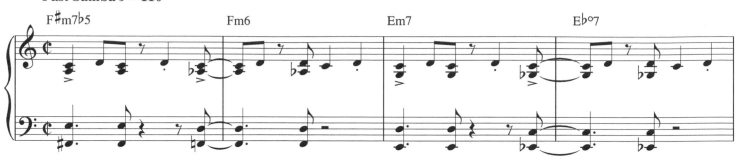

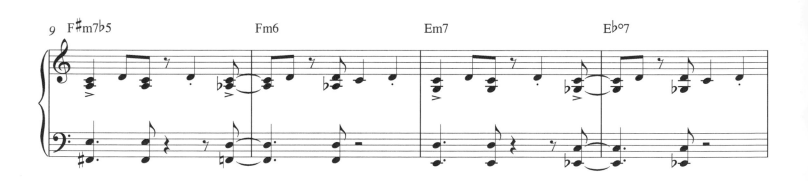

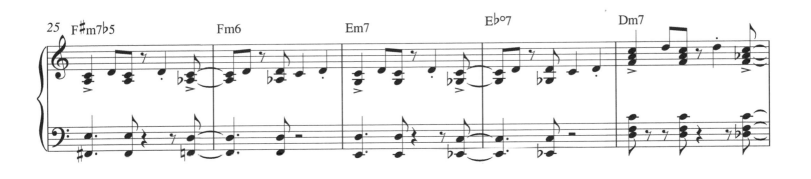

Solo Piano

As with solo Afro-Cuban based piano, playing Brazilian solo piano requires a good sense of independence. The pianist must play melody, comp, and play bass, all at the same time. In order to accomplish this a compromise must be made between the comping and bass parts. Various notes and rhythms have to be left out in order to accommodate each part. Decisions in this regard are often determined by the melody being played at any particular moment. In this solo version of "Bozza Nozza," the left hand plays a continuous bass part while the right hand plays the melody and chords in a bossa rhythm.

Bozza Nozza

TRACK 72

Piano Lead

Medium Bossa ♩ = 154

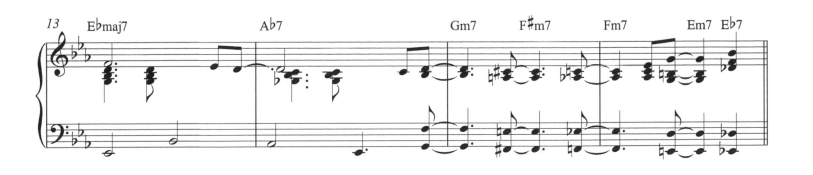

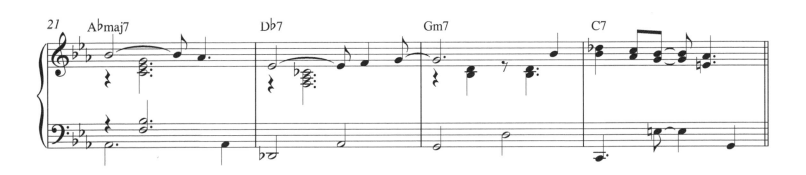

Section 3

LEAD SHEETS AND PLAY ALONG

LEAD SHEETS

All the tunes from this book are written here in lead sheet form. The reader should play these tunes from the lead sheets after studying and playing through the fully written versions in the previous chapters. Characteristic voicings, rhythms, comping patterns, etc. of each style can be used and employed in various ways. The reader should improvise on the tunes as well.

Playing Along with the Audio Tracks

Tracks 73–79 are full band recordings of the lead sheet tunes. The piano is isolated on the left stereo channel and the rest of the band is on the right stereo channel. The reader may listen to the tracks in stereo and then may play along with the band by turning down the left channel. Practice comping during the heads and sax or flute solos, and improvise during the piano solo sections. The reader may turn down the right channel to isolate the piano on the left channel in order to focus on the piano's comping and improvisations. A road map for each of the band tracks follows.

Mamba Mia (Track 73)
Head (sax)
Sax solo: Montuno-32 measures
Piano solo: Montuno-32 measures
Head (sax)
Ending—out at Fine

Bozza Nozza (Track 77)
Head (sax)
Sax solo: one chorus
Piano solo: one chorus
Head (sax)
Ending—measure 33 to end

Alacha (Track 74)
Head (flute)
Flute solo: one chorus
Piano solo: one chorus
Head (flute)
Ending—take second ending

Cosa Nuova (Track 78)
Head (sax)
Sax solo: one chorus
Piano solo: one chorus
Head (sax)
Ending—second ending

Speranza (Track 75)
Head (flute)
Flute solo: one chorus
Piano solo: one chorus
Head (flute)
Ending—measure 45 to end

Samba Maria (Track 79)
Head (flute)
Flute solo: two choruses
Piano solo: two choruses
Head (flute)
Ending—measure 33 to end

Felice Triplice (Track 76)
Head (sax)
Sax solo: three choruses
Piano solo: three choruses
Head (sax)
Ending—last measure

Performers
Bryson Borgstedt: tenor sax, soprano sax, and flute
John Valerio: piano
Tom Hildreth: bass
Rick Dior: drums and percussion

Mamba Mia

Montuno Solo Section
Play 16 times
(32 measures) for each solo

90

Alacha

Felice Triplice

TRACK 76

Bozza Nozza

TRACK 77

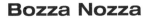

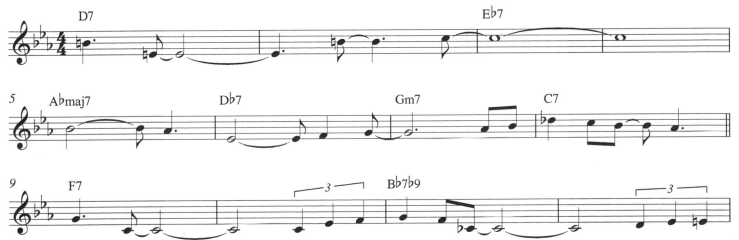

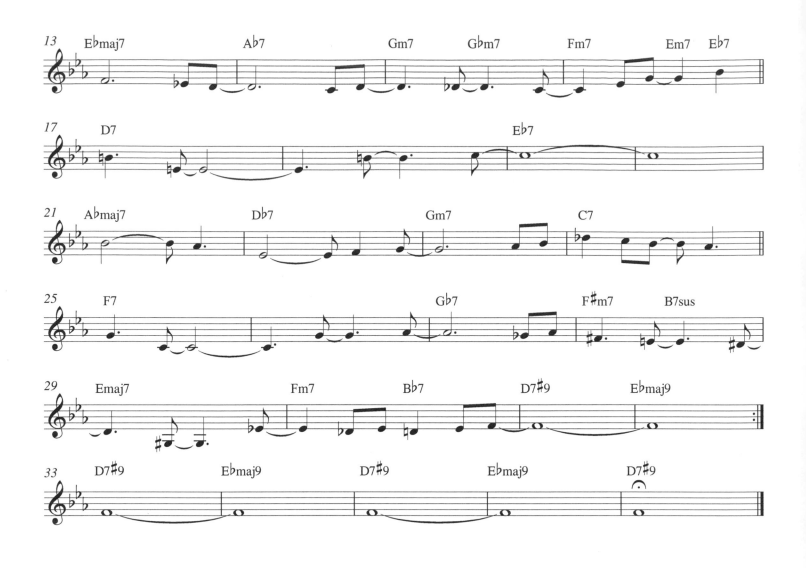

Cosa Nuova

TRACK 78

Fast Bossa ♩ = 200

Samba Maria